7 ^{oo}

5

sharon montrose
Lightweights

Stewart, Tabori & Chang
New York

Published in 2003 by
Stewart, Tabori & Chang
A Company of La Martinière Groupe
115 West 18th Street · New York, NY 10011

Export Sales to all countries except Canada, France,
and French-speaking Switzerland:
Thames and Hudson Ltd.
181A High Holborn · London WC1V 7QX
England

Canadian Distribution:
Canadian Manda Group
One Atlantic Avenue, Suite 105 · Toronto, Ontario M6K 3E7
Canada

Library of Congress Cataloging-in-Publication Data
Montrose, Sharon.
Lightweights / Sharon Montrose
p. cm.
ISBN 1-58479-276-0
1. Dogs--Pictorial works. 2. Puppies--Pictorial works. I. Title.

SF430 .M67 2003
636.7'07'0222--dc21
2002191118

The text of this book was composed in Eatwell Skinny by Chank Diesel
Designed by Sharon Montrose & Sally Ann Field
Printed in Hong Kong

10 9 8 7 6 5 4 3 2

For my brother, David

lightweight: 1 lb. 15 ozs.   WHITE BOXER DANGIE 4 WEEKS OLD

lightweight: 2 lbs. 5 ozs.   FRENCH BULLDOG OSCAR 3 WEEKS OLD

DACHSHUND PEANUT 8 WEEKS OLD

lightweight: 4 lbs. 0 ozs.

lightweight: 3 lbs. 2 ozs.

lightweight: 2 lbs. 8 ozs.

COCKER SPANIEL PEGGY 4 WEEKS OLD

TERRIER MIX ZOEY 5 WEEKS OLD

lightweight: 3 lbs. 7 ozs.

PUG **HANK** 6 WEEKS OLD

lightweight: 2lbs. 12ozs.

lightweight: 7 lbs. 5 ozs.   GERMAN SHEPHERD   BERNARD   5 WEEKS OLD

lightweight: 13 lbs. 2 ozs.

DALMATIAN DAISY 9 WEEKS OLD

lightweight: 1 lb. 2 ozs. BOSTON TERRIER SUGAR 4 WEEKS OLD

WEIMARANERS

SCOOTER

LILY

MINNOW

DUTCH

SALLY

2 WEEKS OLD

combined lightweight: 17 lbs. 3 ozs.

five weeks later...

WEIMARANERS SCOOTER & LILY 7 WEEKS OLD

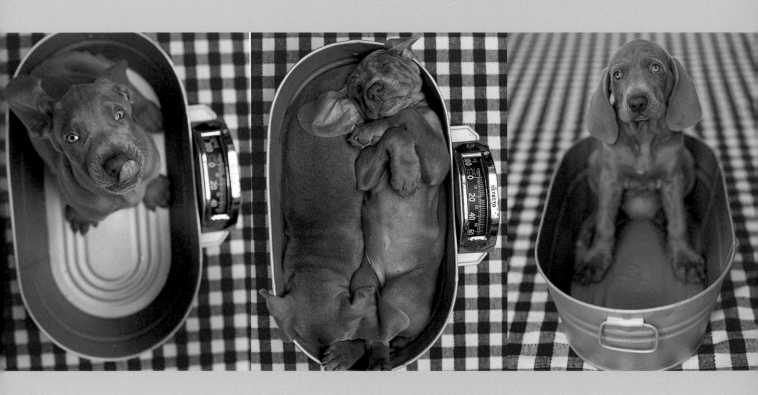

combined lightweight: 22lbs. 6ozs.

lightweight: 2 lbs. 2 ozs.

CHIHUAHUA DOT 4 WEEKS OLD

GOLDEN RETRIEVER SUNNY 9 WEEKS OLD

lightweight: 9 lbs. 11 ozs.

lightweight: 7 lbs. 9 ozs.

BOXER TONKA 7 WEEKS OLD

lightweight: 7 lbs. 5 ozs.

BOXER ARNOLD 5 WEEKS OLD

lightweight: 4 lbs. 9 ozs.

lightweight: 4 lbs. 12 ozs.

BOXER MADDIE 5 WEEKS OLD

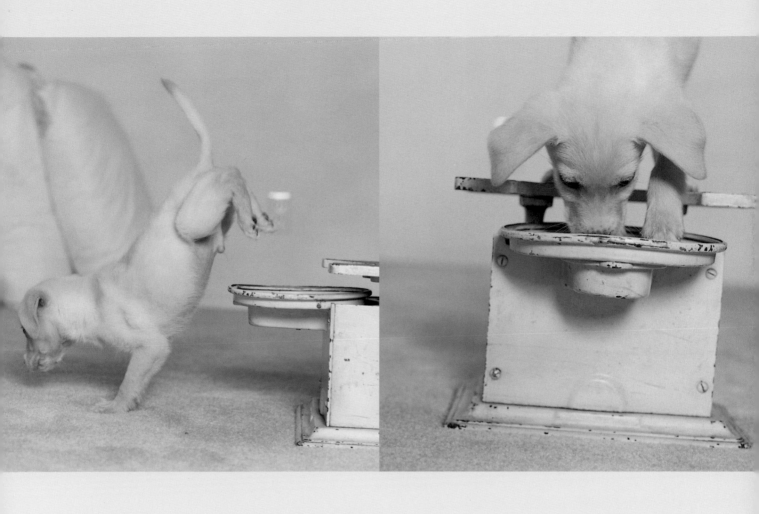

lightweight: 5 lbs. 0 ozs.   LAB MIX PINK 6 WEEKS OLD

lightweight: **6** lbs. 0 ozs.

ENGLISH BULLDOG *CHARLIE* 6 WEEKS OLD

lightweight: 8 lbs. 0 ozs.   BOXER SOPHIE 8 WEEKS OLD

lightweight: **2** lbs. **9** ozs.

SHIHTZU ROXIE 6 WEEKS OLD

lightweight: 16 lbs. 9 ozs.

SIBERIAN HUSKY RED 10 WEEKS OLD

lightweight: 4 lbs. 12 ozs. LAB MIX SADIE 6 WEEKS OLD

lightweight: 0 lbs. 14 ozs.

TEA CUP CHIHUAHUA LOLA 8 WEEKS OLD

lightweight: **14**lbs. 2ozs.

GREAT DANE SHEILA 8 WEEKS OLD

lightweight: 14 lbs. 8 ozs.

GREAT DANE **DUKE** 8 WEEKS OLD

lightweight: **14**lbs. **11**ozs.

lightweight: 15 lbs. 2 ozs.

GREAT DANE ACE 8 WEEKS OLD

lightweight: **13** lbs. **9** ozs.

DALMATIAN CHESTER 9 WEEKS OLD

JACK RUSSELL TERRIER DOUGH 2 WEEKS OLD

lightweight: 0 lbs. 13 ozs.

LONG-HAIRED DACHSHUND DODGER 3 WEEKS OLD

lightweight: **1** lb. **14** ozs.

lightweight: 2 lbs. 12 ozs. RAT TERRIER RUBY 3 WEEKS OLD

lightweight: 5 lbs. 3 ozs.

BEAGLE EMMA 8 WEEKS OLD

CHOCOLATE LAB SCOUT 7 WEEKS OLD

lightweight: 8 lbs. 2 ozs.

lightweight: **16**lbs. 4ozs.

SIBERIAN HUSKY SHASTA 10 WEEKS OLD

CHIHUAHUA TACO 4 WEEKS OLD

lightweight: 2 lbs. 0 ozs.

ENGLISH BULLDOG DOC 3 WEEKS OLD

lightweight: 2 lbs. 11 ozs.

THANK YOU...

WITH MANY THANKS to my mom, Doris Wise Montrose. Also, David Montrose, Fela Wise, Marian Montrose, Jack & Annie Montrose, Hendrick & Sally, Mikel Healey, Elon Schoenholz, Jean Bourget, Mike Kampler, Anne Masterson & the gang at Casa Canine, Jenny Hope, Elizabeth Kaltman, James Lockhart, Joseph Viles, Carisha Gudvi, Bob Weinberg, Sally Ann Field, Vette Dennison, Kyle Thai, Craig Kovacs and everyone at Photo Center, my literary agent, Betsy Amster, and Leslie Stoker and the whole staff at Stewart, Tabori & Chang. Also, all the puppy owners including Noelle Arnzen, Lourdes R. Mares, Veronica De La Cruz, Ronald M. Gagne, Kelly Chaplin, Daniel Sanchez, Jeni Allen, Sarah Mason, Eloy Aranda, Beverly J. Heath, Kimberly M. Chastain, Alice Malson & Kim Beachler, Greg & Shannon Chapman, Lisa Kendrick, Frankie Shack, Jack Beck & Family, Jeff & Allison Morgan, and especially Jamie Hubert. Thank you Jamie! And all the little lightweights for getting back on the scales after jumping off of them!

And most of all, Spencer Starr. Without you, I simply could not have made this book. Your help was invaluable to me. You are invaluable to me. I love you.

Very Special thanks to:

Ramish Venugopal
and everyone at:
the ICON Los Angeles
5450 Wilshire Blvd.
Los Angeles, CA 90036
www.iconla.com

Chank Diesel
www.chank.com

Mamiya America